The Twins Say...
ALWAYS ALWAYS LOVE YOURSELF AND BE HAPPY

Dr. Keesha Karriem

Story & Activity Book

Illustrated By:
Arushan Art

Printed in the United States of America

ISBN 978-1-7372592-0-6 (digital)

ISBN 978-1-7372592-1-3 (paperback)

ISBN 978-1-7372592-2-0 (hardback)

Publisher: Dr. Keesha Karriem

www.drkauthor.com

Dedication

The Twins Say...Always Always Love Yourself and Be Happy was inspired by my beautiful twin nieces Kyaana and Kylila.

This book is dedicated to my amazing son, mom, sister & brother in-law who have always supported me. As my beloved brother Keefe always said: "It is important to know how to read."

Lastly, and most importantly, this book is devoted to all the beautiful Black girls and boys who were ever told that: their skin was too dark, their hair was too nappy, or their lips were too big. This book is for any child or adult bullied about their race or religion; or their physical or mental disability. Please know that you are loved. We can only control our feelings and beliefs. Learning to love yourself despite what others say is the key to being happy.

So, starting today... Always Always Love Yourself and Be Happy!

Special Thanks to:
Veonne Anderson, my publishing coach, Arusha Art, Titus Nixon Photography. KDS, BIG, NFTM, Soros of Zeta Tau Zeta, Brothers of Upsilon Sigma Chapter, Red and my dear family and friends. This book would not be possible without the Grace of Allah.

Self-Love

Care for you
Like you do for others
Care for you
Like a sister or brother

Treat yourself like Royalty
Not just Once or Twice
Treat yourself like a Royalty
Morning, Noon and Night

Take care of Your Body
Take care of your Mind
Always be Grateful
Aways be Genuine & Kind

Remember to Focus
Listen Deep Down Inside
Remember you are Enough
Listen to your Inner Guide

Make a Promise Today
No Matter who you are
To Always Always
Love Yourself
While reaching
for the Stars

Hugging Mommy and Daddy makes us Happy
They say no matter what we do
Always Always love yourself
Always Always be good to you

Auntie says we are Beautiful like Africa
Auntie tells us we are Smart.
To always do our Homework
To always Share and do our Part

My Grandma and Cousin say
Whether you are black or brown
Whether you are a girl or boy
Never forget to wear your crown

Love Yourself
and
Be Happy

Whether you can run or jump
Whether you can hear or speak

Always Always
Love Yourself

Be Happy

Whether you can see or not
Love yourself from your head to feet

When you love yourself
You take care of your health
Everyone should understand
How important it is to wash your hands

In my family, we all love each other
We wear our crowns every day
We are happy with our lives
No matter what people say

10

Everyone around the world should know
Happiness comes from within
Everyone is different and unique
Always, always love the skin you are in

So when you go to bed at night
No matter where you are
Say I love you to yourself
While reaching for the stars

Do You Promise To Always Always Love Yourself?

I, _____

(print your name)

Love Myself Because:

_____

_____

TWINS COLOR AND TRACE
ACTIVITY PAGES

I Love Myself

Mommy Daddy Happy

Auntie and Africa

My Crown

Love Yourself
and
Be Happy

Always Always Love Yourself

Be Happy

Run and Jump

Wash my hands

Children and world

Bed and Sleep

About the Author

"You are the author of your life, love and happiness;
so make it an exciting story!"

- Dr. Keesha L. Karriem, Best-Selling Author

Dr. Keesha L. Karriem was born in Chicago, Illinois. She is the Executive Director of a family-owned business that provides residential care to persons with developmental and intellectual disabilities. As a single mother, aunt, entrepreneur, government worker and college professor she is committed to instilling the principles of Emotional Intelligence (EI). EI among other things, encompasses managing your emotions and self-awareness.

Dr. Karriem obtained her Doctorate Degree from the University of Phoenix and completed her dissertation on Stress and Emotional Intelligence (EI). Her analysis shows how EI contributes to significant life outcomes, such as better decision making and improved learning skills.

After becoming an aunt of two beautiful twin girls she decided to create inspiring books that teach both young and old about Emotional Intelligence, diversity, values: and those with special needs. Dr. Karriem's first book

"The Twins say Always Always Keep your Promises", became an Amazon Best Seller. This book taught children the importance of keeping their promises.

"The Twins say Always Always love Yourself and Be Happy", was created to inspire young children to love the features of their diversity; and to celebrate and be happy about who they are. Dr. Karriem wishes for all children to learn the principle of self-awareness and self-love which encompasses the beauty of their uniqueness.

To order personally signed book copies or to contact Dr. Karriem for book fairs, book signings, or EI webinars: please log onto her website: https://drkauthor.com/